EDINBURGH, GRANTON & LEITH RAILWAYS

KENNETH G. WILLIAMSON

AMBERLEY

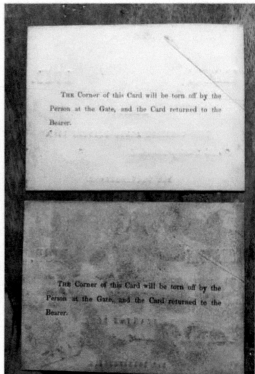

First published 2023

Amberley Publishing
The Hill, Stroud
Gloucestershire, GL5 4EP

www.amberley-books.com

Copyright © Kenneth G. Williamson, 2023

The right of Kenneth G. Williamson to be identified
as the Author of this work has been asserted in
accordance with the Copyrights, Designs and
Patents Act 1988.

ISBN 978 1 3981 0856 1 (print)
ISBN 978 1 3981 0857 8 (ebook)

British Library Cataloguing in Publication Data.
A catalogue record for this book is available from
the British Library.

Typesetting by SJmagic DESIGN SERVICES, India.
Printed in the UK.

Contents

Images

1

Granton Harbour

In the early part of the nineteenth century there was dissatisfaction with the inadequacy of Leith as a port. In 1834 the 5th Duke of Buccleuch, Walter Francis Montagu Douglas Scott, who owned the foreshore at Granton, was approached with a view to constructing a harbour at Granton. The Duke was enthusiastic about this proposal and in 1836 commissioned the development of Granton Harbour.

The eminent civil engineer Robert Stevenson oversaw the construction of the harbour. The construction of the Middle Pier at Granton commenced to Stevenson's design in 1836 with the initial central pier being opened on 28 June 1838, coinciding with the coronation of Queen Victoria. The pier was named Victoria Jetty in her honour before lapsing into simply 'the Middle Pier'.

The opening ceremony was performed by the Duke of Buccleuch's brother, Lord John Scott (MP for Roxburghshire), as the Duke of Buccleuch was in London attending Queen Victoria's coronation. At the time of building, it was one of the largest works ever accomplished in Britain from the unaided resources of a private fortune.

On 1 September 1842, Queen Victoria and Prince Albert landed at Victoria Jetty (pier) on the royal yacht, the *Royal George*, on their first official visit to Scotland. The royal couple were received by the Duke of Buccleuch at Granton and travelled by carriage through Edinburgh to Dalkeith House where they stayed as guests of the Duke.

Victoria Jetty was extended to a total length of 1,700 feet providing a further ten berths with the work being completed in 1844. However, the pier had no protection from the winds blowing up and down the Firth of Forth, so breakwaters were planned.

Construction of the Western Breakwater started in 1842. The Eastern Breakwater was constructed between 1852 and 1863. Both breakwaters were built with locally quarried stone that required little or no maintenance over the years.

By 1845 a steamboat service ran between Stirling and Granton. Sailings to Stirling continued mainly from Leith until 1914 when the Firth of Forth became a restricted area.

Granton became a successful port at the beginning of the twentieth century, the principal imports consisting of butter, wood and esparto grass, which was used in the manufacture of fine paper, while the main exports were coal, coke and patent fuel, the coke being produced at Granton Gas Works which was close by and which had a rail link to the harbour. The esparto grass that came into Granton went either by road or rail to paper mills in Penicuik, Polton, Currie and Balerno. A steam lighter (barge) was also used up until the middle of the 1950s to transfer esparto grass from Granton to Inverkeithing.

In 1909 the Anglo-Saxon Petroleum Co. Ltd built a storage depot at Granton and the import of petroleum products added to the volume of trade.

The fishing fleet grew considerably and an ice house was built in the late nineteenth century to the west of the harbour.

The small shipbreaking business of Malcolm Brechin, which specialised in dismantling small coasters and trawlers, was situated on reclaimed ground in the Western harbour area and was in business from 1932 up until 1965.

Two railway companies served Granton: the Caledonian Railway, which came in from the west in 1861; and the North British Railway, which, after acquiring the Edinburgh, Perth & Dundee Railway in 1862, came in from the east.

At the base of the Middle Pier a railway line was laid in 1862 under an agreement between the Duke of Buccleuch, the CR and the NBR. This section of line was owned by the Duke of Buccleuch and connected with the CR Granton line coming in from the west from Slateford and the NBR line coming in from the east from Trinity Junction.

This new section of line ran across the north side of Granton Square, a site which had previously been occupied by various dock and weighing machine offices.

A single line, belonging to the Duke of Buccleuch (later Granton Harbour Company), was already in place connecting the Middle Pier and the Western Breakwater.

An early view of Granton Harbour.

2
The North British Railway in Granton and Leith

The Edinburgh, Leith & Newhaven Railway was incorporated by an Act of Parliament dated 13 August 1836. In 1839 the original EL&NR route was amended but this mainly affected the Leith branch.

On 31 August 1842 a horse-drawn railway was opened from Scotland Street station to Trinity station where the line terminated. The station served the Chain Pier at Newhaven where there was ready-made passenger and goods traffic for the ferry crossing to and from Fife. To reach the ferry, passengers made their way on foot down a steep path from Trinity station.

The Chain Pier collapsed during a storm in 1898 and was never rebuilt.

In 1844 the EL&NR changed its name to the Edinburgh, Leith & Granton Railway.

On 19 February, 1846 the railway arrived at Granton having been extended westwards by a mile from the original terminus of the EL&NR at Trinity.

Following the extension of the line to Granton a temporary station was opened on Granton Middle Pier, formerly Victoria Jetty, to serve ferry passengers. A more permanent station was opened in the summer of 1848.

The Chain Pier, Trinity, Edinburgh
'destroyed by Storm, Oct. 17, 1898

The Chain Pier (postcard).

Passenger services were withdrawn as a wartime measure from both Granton and Trinity stations on 1 January 1917. The stations reopened on 1 February 1919 but this was just a 'stay of execution' as the final passenger trains ran on 2 November 1925.

Trinity station still stands and has been converted into private houses.

The electric trams, which had arrived in Granton on 3 August 1909, had finally won the battle for passengers.

In May, 1846 the EL&GR Warriston Junction to North Leith line opened.

On 17 May 1847 the EL&GR extended the line south into the heart of Edinburgh with the opening of Scotland Street tunnel that ran directly under the New Town to Canal Street station. The incline was such that cable haulage was required.

On 27 July 1847 the Edinburgh & Northern Railway, which had been incorporated in 1845 to build lines serving Fife and further north, absorbed the EL&GR and Granton Harbour Co.

Although passenger and goods ferries between Granton and Burntisland had been established by Act of Parliament in 1844, one of the main disadvantages was the need to load and unload the rail wagons at either Granton or Burntisland, causing much loss of time and also frequent breakage and damage of goods.

An agreement between the E&NR and the Duke of Buccleuch in 1847 allowed the railway company to build a jetty for the Granton to Burntisland ferry traffic.

On 22 December 1847 the E&NR had drawings made by the engineering firm Hawthorn and Co. of Leith for the building of hydraulic cranes at both Granton and Burntisland piers for loading wagons directly onto the ferries. The 1847 drawings for the cranes at Burntisland still survive and are currently housed within the National Records of Scotland.

The hydraulic crane was invented by Mr William George Armstrong, a Newcastle solicitor, in 1845. He went on to build Newcastle's Swing Bridge and the hydraulic mechanism that operates London's Tower Bridge. The hydraulic system he invented is still in use today. He also went on to found Newcastle University.

However, the proposal to use hydraulic cranes was superseded by the adoption of a 'Floating Railway' devised by Thomas Bouch, who went on to design and build the first Tay Bridge, which collapsed during a storm on Sunday 28 December 1879 with the loss of seventy-five lives.

On 3 February 1850 the world's first seagoing roll-on-roll-off train ferry was introduced between Granton and Burntisland.

The design of the paddle steamer *Leviathan*, built by Robert Napier at Govan on the Clyde in 1849, meant that wagons could be loaded and unloaded directly onto the ferry at any state of the tide by means of a moveable platform on the inclined slips at Granton and Burntisland with a link span extending outwards to the vessel's deck. The wagons being loaded between pier and ferry were controlled by a small stationary steam engine. Foot passengers, however, continued to travel on a separate vessel.

On the opening of the Forth Bridge on 4 March 1890 the train ferries became redundant and were withdrawn, but passenger ferries continued until March 1940.

Parliamentary authority was obtained in 1947 to abandon the Granton–Burntisland ferry.

In 1950 a new service utilising three converted tank landing craft was introduced by Mr John Hall, a Kirkcaldy businessman, but this operation failed three years later and so ended over a century of ferry operations at Granton.

Various attempts have been made to reinstate a ferry service between Granton and Fife over the years but have met with little or no success.

With the opening of the new Queensferry Crossing on 4 September 2017, it is very unlikely that a new ferry service will ever be introduced although there are pleasure cruises sailing to the various islands in the Forth from South Queensferry.

The roll-on-roll-off train ferry designed by Thomas Bouch seen at Burntisland. One of the passenger ferries can be seen in the background.

Under an agreement in 1906 between the NBR, the Duke of Buccleuch and the Commissioners of Northern Lighthouses, the area of slipway formerly used by the Granton–Burntisland ferry boats was used by their lighthouse tenders, various vessels named 'Pharos' being the tender most associated with the Granton base.

Pilotage was based at Leith until the building of a new entrance lock, the construction of which started in the middle of the 1960s. It was then transferred to Granton using fast cutters.

Two hotels were built in Granton to accommodate ferry passengers. The Granton Hotel, which the Duke of Buccleuch commissioned William Burn to design, opened in 1838 for the use of railway travellers before the Forth Bridge was constructed.

The hotel was used as a staging post by ferry passengers as the journey north at this time was by train from Edinburgh Waverley to Granton station, situated on the Middle Pier, and then by ferry to Burntisland in Fife for further rail connections. A second hotel of similar size, designed by John Henderson, was erected at the Burntisland terminus.

In 1939 the Granton Hotel was requisitioned by the Royal Navy and renamed HMS *Claverhouse* in 1940. In post-war years it became a Naval Reserve Centre and today it is an Army Reserve Centre.

On 3 December 2021 a red wheel was placed on the wall of the former Granton Hotel by the National Transportation Trust. The other hotel, which was in Lower Granton Road, was the Wardie Hotel, which has since been converted into residential flats.

On 1 August 1849 the Edinburgh & Northern Railway changed its name to the Edinburgh, Perth & Dundee Railway. The EP&DR fell into the ever-growing NBR net on 29 July 1862.

Both Canal Street station and Scotland Street tunnel were closed on 22 May 1868 when the NBR opened a more easily graded route to Leith and Granton via Abbeyhill and Leith Walk with a connection to the Edinburgh–Berwick line at Piershill Junction. Scotland Street tunnel was only in use for around twenty-one years.

The only station opened on the new line was Leith Walk, which closed in 1930. Further stations were opened at Easter Road (1891–1947), Abbeyhill (1869–1964) and Piershill (1891–1964) on the spur line from Abbeyhill Junction to Piershill Junction.

Powderhall station was the last to be opened in 1895 but had a short life and was closed in 1917 as a result of wartime emergency measures and never reopened. Until recently part of this line was still in use by 'Binliner' trains. Refuse was brought by lorry to the now closed Powderhall Refuse Depot, where it was loaded onto container trains and taken to a landfill site in Dunbar.

Despite the official end of mainline steam in 1968 on British Railways, steam trains still call regularly at Edinburgh Waverley on railtours during the summer months.

Branching off the new NBR line from Abbeyhill, the railway headed east at Bonnington Junction passing Chancelot Flour Mill before dropping under the CR's 1903 Leith New Lines terminating at North Leith (Leith Citadel) station in Commercial Street, Leith. This station opened in 1846 and closed to passengers in 1947.

There were intermediate stations at Bonnington (1846–1947) and Junction Bridge (1869–1947). The latter station was damaged by German incendiary bombs during the Second World War. The original North Leith (Leith Citadel) station building still stands and is now the Citadel Youth Centre.

There was a goods yard at Bonnington (1874–1968) that served the many industries in the area. The line to the goods yard left the mainline just after Bonnington station and swung east crossing Bowling Green Street. There was a north and south yard connected by a bridge over the Water of Leith. A piece of original rail can still be seen in Anderson Place, Leith, where there was a connection from the south yard into a Sugar Bond.

The NBR secured a route into South Leith following the purchase of the antiquated Edinburgh and Dalkeith Railway in 1845 for £113,000. The E&DR's 4-foot 6-inch gauge was subsequently converted into the standard 4-foot 8 ½-inch gauge.

The E&DR was still known as the 'Innocent Railway' even after its acquisition by the NBR, owing to the fact that throughout its independent existence no person had ever been killed on the line.

The E&DR, which had been incorporated in 1826, was a horse-operated railway laid for the conveyance of coal from the Lothian pits to Edinburgh.

Under powers secured in 1834 passenger services were introduced on the E&DR and, like the mineral and goods services, was also horse-operated.

At every station there was a noticeboard forbidding drivers to stop by the way to feed their horses. A journey over the line must have been a very leisurely affair as the average speed was 8 mph and the trains would stop for any passengers in sight.

There were no booking offices on the E&DR and no tickets were ever issued as the passengers clambered aboard knowing that the fare would be collected by the guard.

At a Parliamentary enquiry regarding the non-issue of tickets the managers of the E&DR complained 'many people will not tell where they are going, while others are even more irritating by being unable to decide on their destination!'

Under the original Acts for the railway, steam locomotives were prohibited, so locomotives did not make their appearance on the former E&DR until 1859, some fourteen years after the acquisition of the railway by the NBR.

The ex-E&DR South Leith station closed on 1 July 1903 following the opening of Leith Central station on this date.

As the demand for coal increased the NBR built a series of new lines (due mainly to coal owner's pressure to improve the movement of coal) connecting Leith Docks and the Mid and East Lothian coalfields on 2 January 1915. These lines were known as the Lothian Lines and were used exclusively for coal trains.

With the onset of the First World War and the increased demand for coal these lines proved invaluable as they avoided the choke point at Portobello.

In 1923 coal exports at Leith peaked, but with a post-war decline in coal traffic continuing the Lothian Lines eventually closed in 1967.

3

The Caledonian Railway in Edinburgh, Granton and Leith

The Caledonian Railway entered Edinburgh from Carstairs on 15 February 1848; its terminus was a one-platform station named Lothian Road.

The CR was the first railway to offer direct travel without the need to change trains between Edinburgh and England. Passengers on the CR's great rival, the North British Railway, had to cross the River Tweed at Berwick on foot to continue their rail journey to England.

In 1869 a line was opened from Carfin through Shotts, giving the CR a shorter route between Edinburgh and Glasgow. A locomotive depot was established at Dalry Road, Edinburgh, a short distance from the Lothian Road station.

In 1856 the Caledonian Railway entered into an agreement with the Duke of Buccleuch to build a line to his harbour at Granton financed on a 50/50 basis but operated by the Caledonian Railway.

In 1857 the CR obtained an Act authorising the building of a line from Granton Junction on their ill-fated Haymarket branch to Breakwater Junction. The CR had hoped to connect the Haymarket branch with the Edinburgh & Glasgow Railway at Haymarket but the Directors of the E&GR rejected this proposal and the line was used to serve local industries instead. The former CR branch line was eventually connected at Haymarket in 1964.

The E&GR was absorbed by the NBR on 1 August 1865.

The traffic potential of the docks at Granton and Leith led to branch line extensions while residential development encouraged further branch lines into what became the suburbs of Edinburgh.

On 29 August 1861 the Granton branch opened as a single line for goods and mineral traffic only. With the arrival of the CR, this provided Granton with a direct link to the coalfields and industrial areas of West Lothian and Lanarkshire.

The line to Granton left the CR main line at Slateford Junction and headed north-east through the Gorgie area of the city passing under Slateford Road and across Gorgie Road before turning north at Granton Junction in the Dalry area to cross the ex-E&GR (NBR) main line at Haymarket Central Junction before passing over the Corstorphine Road at Murrayfield and winding through Craigleith towards Granton.

The original 1861 stone arch bridge leading to Murrayfield station was replaced by a wrought-iron girder bridge in 1899 to allow Edinburgh's double-deck cable-hauled trams, some of which were open-top, to pass underneath without decapitating passengers and dislodging hats, especially those worn by ladies at this time.

Overhead electric wires were installed in 1923 when Edinburgh converted its cable-hauled trams to electric trams following the amalgamation with Leith in 1920. Leith's electric tram system had been in operation since 1905.

The CR's Granton branch actually ended in a 'fork', with one line going down on a steep slope towards the Western Breakwater, the other to a goods and mineral station with access (via the lines of the Duke of Buccleuch) to the Middle Pier at Granton, upon which the EP&DR (NBR) was already established.

Having arrived at Granton the CR Directors turned their thoughts to reaching Leith and in 1862 the CR obtained an Act for a line from Crew Junction to the Western Docks at Leith.

In 1863 the CR bought out the Duke of Buccleuch's share and acquired full control of the line to Granton, which was then doubled.

On 1 September 1864 the Leith branch opened for goods and mineral traffic only. At the same time a spur was opened at Dalry allowing through running of trains from Lothian Road to Granton and Leith.

This line turned west then north-west, crossing Dalry Road to connect with the line coming in from Slateford at Coltbridge Junction just before the bridge taking the line over the ex-E&GR (NBR) Edinburgh–Glasgow line at Haymarket Central Junction.

On 3 July 1876 the Western Dalry branch opened allowing CR trains access to the NBR lines at Haymarket West Junction, thus giving the CR running powers over their rival's lines and access to Stirling, Perth and the north. This line was closed on 9 March 1964.

On 1 July 1879 the Leith branch was opened for passenger service.

The original 1848 CR station at Lothian Road was replaced by a new station called Princes Street station, opened on 2 May 1870. The CR had considered making arrangements with the NBR to use Waverley station but the NBR were hostile to the idea.

The new Princes Street station may have been satisfactory when first opened but soon proved inadequate as passenger traffic levels increased. The new station also provoked numerous complaints from the public for its appearance and general shabbiness.

In June 1890 the station, which had been built of timber with a pitched slated roof, suffered a major blaze.

Plans had already been made for a new station and between 1890 and 1893 a new spacious station at Princes Street, known locally as the 'Caley', was erected at a cost of £250,000. The new station came into use in 1894.

In 1899 work started on building a hotel above the station, this opened in 1903 under the name of the Caledonian Railway Princes Street Station Hotel. The hotel has since been renamed and is now called the Waldorf Astoria Edinburgh.

On the branch line to Granton and Leith there were stations at Dalry Road (1900–62), Murrayfield (1879–1962) and Craigleith (1879–1962).

At Craigleith Junction a line branched north-west to serve stations at Barnton Gate (name changed to Davidson's Mains on 1 April 1903) and Cramond Brig (name changed to Barnton on 1 April 1903), both of which opened on 1 March 1894.

A halt was opened at House o' Hill east of Davidson's Mains on 1 February 1937 to serve the expanding housing developments being built in the area. The spread of private cars and local bus services took its toll on many of Edinburgh's suburban rail services and as a consequence of this, the stations on the Barnton branch closed on 7 May 1951.

Goods traffic was handled on the Barnton branch as far as Davidson's Mains until 31 May 1960. The former goods yard is now a supermarket car park.

At Crew Junction (spelt this way so as not to be confused with Crewe Junction in England) the line to Granton branched off to the north while the line to Leith turned eastward.

Continuing on the Leith section of the line there were stations at Granton Road, Newhaven and Leith North (terminus), all of which opened on 1 July 1879. When the latter station was opened it was simply known as Leith but was renamed North Leith on 1 August 1903 after the opening of the NBR's Leith Central station and then Leith North on 7 April 1952.

A halt was also opened on the Leith line at East Pilton on 1 December 1934 to serve the expanding housing developments in the area.

All these stations closed in 1962, a decision which appears very short sighted now.

Crew Junction was an important exchange yard, dealing with traffic going to and from the NBR system at Granton as well as from Granton Harbour and Granton Gas Works.

Immediately north of Crew Junction, Ferry Road was crossed by two separate bridges, the westernmost bridge carrying the Granton branch and the easternmost bridge carrying the Leith branch. Both bridges were replaced by a single bridge when Ferry Road was widened but in November 1999 this bridge was removed and replaced with a pedestrian-only bridge across Ferry Road.

An information board giving a brief history of the railway has been placed beside the pedestrian bridge.

The only station building still extant on the line is Newhaven station, which has been converted into offices

On 5 May 1958 the Edinburgh Princes Street to Leith North passenger services were dieselised. On 28 April 1962 the Edinburgh Princes Street to Leith North passenger services ceased. On 30 April 1962 all the stations on the line were closed.

However, nearly six months after closure, on 16 October 1962, the very last passenger train ran from Leith North, where a temporary platform was erected, to convey King Olav V of Norway, who had arrived by ship at Leith Docks on a state visit to Princes Street station where he was met by the Queen and Duke of Edinburgh. This was the first ever royal state visit to the United Kingdom that did not include London. It was Princes Street station's step-free access which commended arrival there, not that there remained any former NBR railway stations in Leith which could have conveyed the King to Edinburgh.

On 7 September 1964 the former CR Haymarket branch (Duff Street siding) was eventually connected to the ex-E&GR (NBR) at Haymarket. On 5 September 1965 Edinburgh Princes Street station closed completely.

The CR built a station at Granton Gas Works that opened on 27 February 1903 for the sole use of the workers as there was no transport links to the Gas Works at this time. Granton Gas Works station did not appear in the published timetables but apparently local residents as well as the workers used the trains.

The station was closed by the LMS in 1942 as transport links improved as housing was built in the surrounding area. The site of the old Gas Works is now occupied by Edinburgh College and a supermarket. The line into Granton Gas Works came off the CR's 1861 Granton branch.

The station building has a Category B listing and is currently being redeveloped by Edinburgh Council at a cost of 4.75 million pounds. Once the work has been completed it will be managed by WASPS (Workshops & Artists Studio Provisions Scotland Ltd). On completion, the redevelopment will provide office and flexible work spaces for the creative, charity and social enterprise sectors. The new development is being called Granton Station Creative Works, notwithstanding the original Granton Station (ex-NBR) was on the Middle Pier at Granton and was closed along with Trinity station in 1925 by the LNER. However, whatever the name, rightly or wrongly, the refurbished station is given, it's great to see it being brought back to life and being put to good use.

The journey time, according to a 1907 working timetable, was twelve minutes from Princes Street station (the 'Caley') to Granton Gas Works.

Granton Gas Works had its own fleet of locomotives for shunting coal wagons within the works, both standard gauge and 2-foot gauge.

The former CR's goods station and yard at Granton closed on 5 February 1968. However, the original station building and yard are still in situ and are today occupied by William Waugh, Scrap Merchant. This building and Granton Gas Works station are the last remnants of the Caledonian Railway's 1861 line to Granton.

The last trains to use the former CR Granton branch were oil trains which served the Texaco Oil Terminal situated behind the old Gas Works station at the former Breakwater Junction. This service ended in the 1980s.

This large tank farm was built in 1959 by the Regent Oil Co. Ltd (Texaco), which brought fairly large tankers, of their time, to the Western harbour.

The original wharves along the Western Breakwater, which were built of timber, began to fall into disrepair during the 1950s and were gradually abandoned. The last section to go was the tanker berth at the outer end of the breakwater. The last coastal tanker called in 1985.

Part of the former railway line from Crew Junction to Granton has been realigned to make way for a new road called West Granton Access. The remains of the original CR line from Breakwater Junction to Granton can still be seen but is not accessible. The line to Leith follows the original route and is now a very popular cycle path/walkway.

4

The North British Railway's Leith Central Station and the Caledonian Railway's 1903 Leith New Lines

The North British Railway's determination to keep its great rival, the Caledonian Railway, from gaining a foothold in Leith saw it make the decision in 1891 to build a short branch line northward from Abbeyhill to a new station at the foot of Leith Walk in central Leith, notwithstanding that in 1884 the NBR had informed Leith Town Council that a further line to Leith was not viable.

Leith Central and its branch did not result from a separate Act of Parliament but was created out of a subsidiary Schedule to the Waverley Station Extension Act of 1891.

Contracts to build the line were not let until the end of 1897 and it wasn't until 1 July 1903 that Leith Central was opened for passenger traffic with trains running every thirty minutes on the six minutes of journey time to the Waverley.

The change of mind by the NBR to build a line to central Leith was made as the CR, passed by an Act of Parliament on 4 July 1890, proposed building an elevated line across Leith from Newhaven Junction to Seafield for both passenger and goods traffic. The CR also proposed building a passenger-only line from Princes Street station ('Caley') below Princes Street to a station at Waterloo Place, then by tunnel through Calton Hill to Abbeyhill and then to continue to Lochend to join the CR's original route from Newhaven Junction to Seafield. This scheme was opposed by Edinburgh Town Council, the NBR and was rejected by Parliament.

In 1891 the CR further proposed the formation of a new railway company, the Edinburgh & Leith Junction Railway involving both the CR and NBR. The route planned was to diverge at the NBR's Haymarket station and run below West Maitland Street and Shandwick Place with a spur linking in from the CR's Princes Street station. From the West End of Edinburgh, the line was to proceed below Charlotte Square, George Street, St James Square (station) and then continue by way of a tunnel through Calton Hill to Abbeyhill and Lochend as per the first scheme.

The Joint Line was to have three outlets from a triangular Junction at Lochend:

1. Facing west onto the proposed CR line across Leith.
2. Facing east onto the same line.
3. Facing east onto the NBR line south of Lochend Loch between Easter Road and Piershill stations.

This scheme was also rejected.

Having again been rebuffed the CR decided to proceed with the original Newhaven Junction to Seafield scheme that had been approved by Parliament. This was originally a goods-only line but stations were commenced at Ferry Road and Leith Walk.

The line opened on 1 August 1903 and was known as the Caledonian Railway's 1903 Leith New Lines.

From Newhaven Junction the line swung south-eastwards through Victoria Park to pass below Ferry Road. After passing Ferry Road the line passed in a shallow cutting between Gosford Place and Connaught Place with Chancelot Flour Mill on the west side, which had a rail connection to the CR. The line crossed the NBR's junction at Bonnington East and the Water of Leith by a series of bridges and viaducts. The line then made a 90 per cent turn east crossing the road junction diagonally at Bonnington Toll on the first of three massive lattice girder bridges that were to become a distinctive feature of the line. Still on an embankment, the line ran along the north side of the grounds of Pilrig House.

Robert Louis Stevenson's grandfather was born in Pilrig House, which is featured in Stevenson's novel *Catriona*. Pilrig House still exists and has been converted into residential flats.

A temporary halt was built in Pilrig Park for a Royal Volunteer Review by His Majesty King Edward VII held on Monday 18 September 1905. Little did the men know that within nine years they would be called to war.

The junction for Leith Walk West Goods Yard diverged just to the north of Pilrig Park as the line turned south-east again. The entrance to the goods yard was off Leith Walk opposite Leith Tram Depot.

The banana company Fyffes had, for many years, operated a depot at Leith Walk West. Craig & Rose, paint manufacturers, suppliers of paint for the Forth Bridge, whose premises in Leith Walk lay adjacent, also used the goods yard. The paint went by rail to Leith Docks. From there it was sent by ship to their distribution centre at Dartford in England. The goods yard was rail connected until 6 May 1968.

As the line approached Leith Walk the embankment gave way to a stone arched viaduct beside Jane Street before crossing Leith Walk on the second of the lattice girder bridges. From the east side of Leith Walk to Easter Road the line was carried on a further series of masonry arches that can still be seen in Manderston Street. It was on this section of the line that work on Leith Walk passenger station was started but never fully completed.

Easter Road was then crossed by the third girder bridge. Beyond Easter Road the line turned south-east again and continued on an embankment past Robert Younger & Co.'s St Ann's Maltings before swinging round a further 90 per cent to cross over the NBR's Leith Central branch at Hawkhill Avenue and then under Lochend Road.

There was a goods yard and mineral station on the section of line between Lochend Road and Restalrig Road. The only traffic the yard appears to have handled was timber from James Walker & Co. Ltd, timber merchants, who eventually purchased the yard and surrounding land.

From Restalrig Road overbridge the line continued eastwards in a deep cutting before swinging round north-west to the junction serving South Leith Goods and Seafield Yard. The South Leith Goods line swung round to the west and ran parallel to Seafield Road on an embankment with a high stone retaining wall next to the road, leading to an arched viaduct, which can still be seen today, before crossing over Seafield Place. The entrance to Seafield Cemetery was crossed on an ornamental girder bridge with a similar-type overbridge across Seafield Place.

After traversing another short length of embankment between Leith Links and Salamander Street the line fanned out into South Leith Goods and Mineral Depot, which had facilities for dealing with all types of goods.

A substantial brick- and slate-roofed goods transfer building was provided in the depot with a two-storey office block fronting Bath Street. Sidings in the yard served several private traders. One siding crossed Bath Street on the level to serve the biscuit factory of William Crawford & Sons.

The goods yard was renamed Leith East in 1952.

The line serving Seafield Yard crossed Seafield Road and the NBR line on a long plate girder bridge before descending into extensive reception sidings on land reclaimed from the sea beyond the eastern end of Leith Docks.

The CR also built a brick engine shed, having two roads, a timber coaling bench and a 60-foot-diameter turntable.

The land acquisition and construction costs for the line to Leith Docks proved to be enormous for the CR while on completion the goods traffic turned out be meagre and the anticipated coal traffic from the central coalfields to Leith for shipment never materialised, resulting in the whole project becoming something of a 'white elephant' for the CR. The sidings were underused and it is questionable if the engine shed was ever used by the CR to stable locomotives.

Meanwhile the NBR, who had the monopoly on the coal traffic from the Mid and East Lothian coalfields, were desperate to acquire additional land to expand their siding capacity at Seafield.

In 1912 the CR entered into an agreement with the NBR to sell an area of ground extending to some 5.5 acres at Seafield that was surplus to requirements for £20,000 and to lease under a separate agreement the locomotive depot for a payment of £200 per annum. However, the fabric of both the engine shed and coaling bench had fallen into disrepair and the NBR intimated that they were not prepared to take it on until the shed etc., had been repaired. The repair work was eventually carried out, paid for by the CR, and the NBR took possession of the facilities in 1916.

Up until 1916 there had been no direct connection between the NBR and the CR lines at Seafield but as part of the NBR Lothian Railways Bill of 1915, a project to speed the traffic flow of coal between the collieries and Leith Docks, a line (Railway No. 3 in the scheme) was proposed to run from the north-west end of the new NBR marshalling yard at Craigentinny to a junction with the CR's Leith New Lines some 20 yards from the south abutment of the bridge across Seafield Road and the NBR lines into South Leith yard.

Again, it is doubtful if the NBR ever got round to working engines off Seafield shed as access from South Leith to the shed was by a somewhat roundabout route. The line appeared to be seldom used by either the NBR or its successor, the LNER, the latter company deciding to sever the junction with the former CR, now LMSR, line on 15 October 1929.

The brick signal box that had been built by the CR to control the junction and which opened for traffic on 13 March 1916 was closed and subsequently demolished.

It wasn't until May 1945 that the LNER brought the engine shed and its facilities at Seafield into use, mainly to ease the congestion and smoke nuisance at St Margaret's, their principal freight locomotive depot in Edinburgh. This, of course, necessitated the reinstatement of the junction at Seafield Road which was then controlled by a ground frame with track circuiting being the method of working used for locomotives between Meadows Yard and Seafield loco depot.

From May 1945 until its closure in BR days on 13 October 1962 Seafield depot proved to be a useful outstation of St Margaret's for locomotives engaged on freight and mineral traffic duties from the Meadows and South Leith yards.

The junction between the LNER and LMSR lines at Seafield was never considered to be a major part of traffic exchange between the two railway companies, but it was used on occasion in BR days.

With the rationalisation of freight lines to Leith in early 1966, the Newhaven Junction to Leith Walk West goods depot section was closed on 4 January 1966 resulting in Leith East goods depot and Leith Walk West goods depot being accessed from Meadows Yard to Seafield Junction. There the track layout had to be altered to connect into the line to Leith East, which had made an almost 90-degree turn to the west, south of Seafield Junction, to run alongside Seafield Road on a high embankment with sandstone retaining walls before crossing Seafield Place on an over bridge and descending into the spacious Leith East goods yard.

Leith Walk West depot only lasted a further two-plus years, closing on 6 May 1968 while Leith East depot lasted a further five years, closing on 31 December 1973, so bringing to an end the last remnant of the CR's Leith New Lines.

The CR had goods yards at Newhaven and Bonnington (Rosebank), which closed on 25 March 1965.

When the Leith New Lines opened in 1903, a suburban service from Edinburgh to Seafield was intended. At Newhaven station an additional platform was built for the new line. Platforms were also built at Ferry Road and Leith Walk.

Despite the platforms being built at Ferry Road and Leith Walk, the stations were never fully completed. The reason for this was the CR, in securing Leith Town Council's support for the line through Leith, guaranteed never to charge more for the Edinburgh–Leith fare than their rivals, the NBR. This was a disastrous decision as the NBR line from Abbeyhill to Leith Central station was a fraction of the length of the CR line and much less costly to build as it did not involve elevated sections. That the new CR line never carried timetabled passenger traffic came as no surprise.

A planned connection from the CR Seafield line to the NBR Leith Central line was never built.

In 1917 one set of rails of the double track on the Leith New Lines was lifted for use in France.

The Leith New Lines were a bold venture by the CR to establish itself, not only in Leith, then one of Scotland's busiest ports, but also the Mid and East Lothian coalfields, but the scheme was doomed to failure from the start and it is a wonder that the line lasted as long as it did.

The eventual construction of Leith Central station by the NBR saw the largest station ever constructed in Britain from scratch in the twentieth century. The station was much larger than necessary and as such was never used to its full potential. Although the actual branch line was only 1 mile long, it was twelve years before the line and the new station was completed.

The very much understated opening of Leith Central, a large four-platform terminus, took place on 1 July 1903. Passengers had difficulty in finding the entrance to the station as the NBR hadn't put up any signage. The only destination originally being offered was to Waverley station in Edinburgh.

Despite the trials and tribulations of getting the line to Leith, the station became quite popular, mainly due to the 'Pilrig Muddle' on the tramway system where passengers had to change trams from the electrically operated Leith trams to the cable-operated system of Edinburgh at Pilrig on the boundary between Edinburgh and Leith.

However, on 22 June 1923 the 'muddle' came to an end when the Edinburgh system was electrified and through-running by electric tram from Edinburgh to Leith became possible following the amalgamation of Edinburgh and Leith in 1920. Inevitably, Leith Central began to lose passengers mainly because of the inconvenient public access, the notorious Waverley Steps at the Waverley end, and so started a thirty-one-year decline.

The station was used to bring back the remains of soldiers, many of who came from Leith, of the 7th Battalion, the Royal Scots, Leith Territorial Battalion based in Dalmeny Street, Leith. They perished in Britain's worst railway disaster, which occurred outside the CR signal box at Quintinshill near Gretna on 22 May 1915.

The funeral train left Carlisle and travelled up to Edinburgh on the NBR's Waverley Route, arriving at Leith Central station. There was a funeral procession from Dalmeny Street that proceeded up Leith Walk to Rosebank Cemetery, where the men were laid to rest in a corner almost on the boundary of Edinburgh and Leith.

In 1937 there was a fire at the station, and although it caused some damage, the two platforms that survived proved sufficient for the amount of services the station provided.

As part of the original scheme for the NBR branch to Leith it was proposed to build a station at Hawkhill with interchange facilities with the CR line, so creating a northern suburban circle. This never came to fruition but on 8 April 1950 Easter Road Park Halt, a single platform, was opened to serve Easter Road Football Stadium, the home of Hibernian Football Club.

The halt remained open until January 1964, although it wasn't officially closed until 24 July 1967. While incoming trains stopped directly outside the football stadium, return trains left from Abbeyhill station, which meant rival fans walking up Easter Road to Abbeyhill. On 5 April, 1952 Leith Central branch and station closed to passengers.

Following a surprisingly short working career, work was started in 1955 to convert Leith Central into what was probably Britain's first diesel depot to maintain DMUs, which were being introduced on a dieselised Edinburgh Waverley–Glasgow Queen Street service. Platforms were removed and fuel tanks installed.

Given that there was no real opposition to the conversion of the station to a maintenance depot shows how little regard British Railways and indeed the general public had for the station 'nobody wanted'.

As the early diesels had no fuel gauges the fuel tanks were allowed to fill to overflowing. With the depot being one storey above street level, this led, not surprisingly, to a number of cases of 'rising damp' in some of the shops below the station.

I have a personal interest in Leith Central station as my grandmother's cousin James (Jimmy) Gordon was the station foreman at Leith Central. He retired in 1965 after working forty-four years on the NBR, LNER and BR. He also fought in the First World War as a private in the Gordon Highlanders.

He was an accomplished artist and lived in the former Edinburgh & Dalkeith Railway station in Constitution Street, which closed to passengers on 1 July 1903 following the opening of Leith Central station. Many of his paintings could be seen hanging on the walls of pubs in Leith. Sadly, the old E&DR station was demolished not long after he and his fellow neighbours moved out. Jimmy Gordon died in 1986 and is buried in Caddonfoot Cemetery in Clovenfords in the Scottish Borders.

The closure of Leith Central took place in 1972 and the empty station lay vacant for around seventeen years before the train shed was finally demolished in 1989. The site is now occupied by a supermarket and soft play centre.

Leith Central in its ruined state was unusual in inspiring Irvine Welsh's controversial book *Trainspotting*.

Very little remains of Leith Central station and the branch line from Abbeyhill.

The former CR Newhaven station building still exists and, as previously mentioned, is now offices. The station building can be seen in Craighall Road and the platforms from the cycle path/walkway running directly underneath the station.

The former NBR Bonnington station at Newhaven Road is now a private dwelling house. The platforms still exist and can be seen from the cycle path/walkway down to Leith.

There is still quite a lot of the elevated section of the former CR's ill-fated 1903 Leith New Lines from Newhaven Junction to Seafield still standing. The remains of viaducts as well as Leith Walk station can still be seen in Jane Street and Manderston Street, Leith, respectively.

There is a cycle path/walkway beginning just off the foot of Easter Road called the Restalrig Railway Path, which follows the former CR line passing under the bridges at Lochend and Restalrig on its way down to Leith Links.

New footbridges take the walkway across the entrance to Seafield Cemetery and Seafield Place to Leith Links.

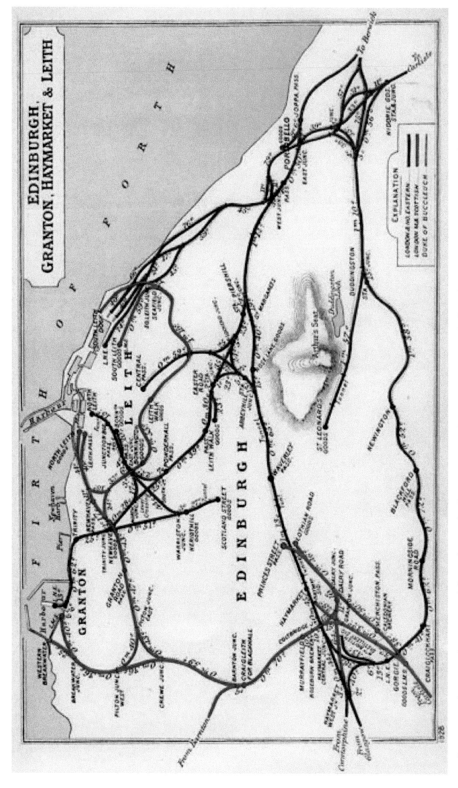

Railway map showing the extent of the railways, both CR/LMS and NBR/LNER, in Edinburgh, Granton, Haymarket and Leith in 1928.

Scotland Street – Granton – London Road Junction – Abbeyhill – Edinburgh Waverley (North British Railway)

Scotland Street goods yard seen in NBR days. Heriothill tunnel can be seen in the background.

A view of Scotland Street coal yard.

Scotland Street tunnel, built 1847 and closed 1868. The tunnel was used in various enterprises before finally being closed off. The tunnel can still be seen today and the former goods yard is now called 'The Yard' and is an adventure play centre for disabled children, young people and their families.

Heriothill tunnel with Broughton Street and Rodney Street above. This is now part of a cycle path/walkway down to Leith.

The original Edinburgh, Leith & Granton Railway bridge built in 1841 over the Water of Leith at Warriston Road.

Trinity Station (closed 1925) on the former NBR line to Granton. This station incorporated two unusual items of interest. One was a small dial linked to a windvane showing the direction of the wind, presumably for the information of intending ferry passengers. The other was the provision of a small moveable pane at the base of one of the windows through which tickets were sold to fishwives, no doubt to keep the main booking hall clear of the odour of fish. On the trains, special vehicles were provided for the fishwives for the same purpose.

Another view of Trinity station looking towards Granton.

BR 0-6-0 Class J37 (ex-NBR) No. 64624 is seen at Trinity station on a railtour on 31 August 1963.

Granton Hotel as seen in 1907. Note the lack of trams as they did not reach Granton until 3 August 1909.

Official invitation to the opening of the Forth Bridge on 4 March 1890.

NBR 4-4-0T No. 78 (solid bogie wheels) is seen at Granton Harbour station with a train for Edinburgh.

Another view of Granton Harbour station, which the LNER closed permanently to passengers in 1925.

BR 0-6-0T Class J88 (ex-NBR) No. 68340 is seen with a loaded timber train coming off the Middle Pier at Granton.

BR 0-6-2T Class N15 (ex-NBR) No. 69187 is seen shunting at Granton in BR days.

BR 0-6-0 Class J36 (ex-NBR) No. 65334 is seen passing the Middle Pier at Granton on 4 November 1955 having just come off the ex-CR Granton line.

BR 4MT 2-6-0 (ex-LMS) No. 43133 is seen crossing the entrance to the Middle Pier at Granton on 2 May 1955 heading west.

On 27 August 1970 there was a head-on collision on the Granton line between two BR Class 40 diesels, No. 368 and No. 363. Fortunately, both crews escaped with minor injuries. The picture shows the substantial damage done to loco No. 386.

Trinity Junction as seen in September 1967. The former CR line to Leith North crossed over the ex-NBR junction at this point. Today this junction is a cycle path/walkway with very little trace of any of the railways that once ran here.

A pair of BR Clayton Type diesels and brake van are seen passing under the ex-CR Leith line at Trinity Junction. This class of very much under-powered diesels replaced the steam locomotives that previously hauled coal trains to Granton destined for Granton Gas Works.

NBR Powderhall station, 1910 (closed 1917).

A view looking north of former NBR Powderhall station with Chancelot Flour Mill, which was destroyed by fire, in the background.

All that remains today of ex-NBR Powderhall station.

A 'Binliner' train is seen arriving at Powderhall Refuse Depot, which is now closed, on the original NBR line to Granton. The EWS Class 67021 diesel will run round the train and push the empty wagons towards the depot. The wagons will then be winched into position by a stationary engine ready for loading.

The next station after Powderhall was Leith Walk station. This is a view of the station looking east.

Another view of Leith Walk station, this time looking north. The station was closed in 1930.

The entrance at Easter Road to Leith Walk goods yard.

BR 0-6-0 Class J37 (ex-NBR) No. 64624 is seen at Easter Road station at the head of a railtour on 31 August 1963.

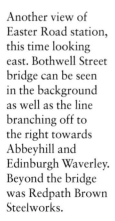

Another view of Easter Road station, this time looking east. Bothwell Street bridge can be seen in the background as well as the line branching off to the right towards Abbeyhill and Edinburgh Waverley. Beyond the bridge was Redpath Brown Steelworks.

A colour view of Easter Road signal box.

The signal box at London Road Junction, 21 March 1971. Rossie Place and Easter Road can be seen in the background. Although I was brought up in Granton and went to school there, I spent a lot of time with my grandmother who lived in Rossie Place. From her top corner flat there was an unfettered view of the railway lines to Granton, Leith Central, Lochend Junction as well as Redpath Brown Steelworks. There were many other industries in the area at this time, sadly now all gone.

Right: London Road Junction showing lines going to Leith Central, Lochend Junction as well as to Granton.

Below: Abbeyhill station looking south. I was a trainspotter at this station as a boy. I became friendly with the stationmaster, who showed me a secret way to access and exit the station if he was not on duty and the station was locked. Stopping trains passed through this station as well as empty coaching stock heading back to Craigentinny. The spur connected with the East Coast Mainline at Piershill Junction just east of St Margaret's Engine Shed.

Another view of
Abbeyhill station, this
time looking north,
September 1967.

A very old view of the
east end of Waverley
station.

The east end of
Edinburgh Waverley
today. I may add,
the cows seen in the
background are not
real!

Edinburgh Waverley station Up main platform looking west around 1912.

BR 5MT B1 4-6-0 loco No. 61242 on a passenger train is seen at platform 7 in Edinburgh Waverley.

Ex-LNER now BR A2 4-6-2 Pacific loco No. 60510 *Robert the Bruce* is seen waiting to depart from the west end of Edinburgh Waverley.

BR 2MT
2-6-0 loco No.
78049 arrives
at Edinburgh
Waverley covered
in snow.

BR 2-6-2T loco
No. 67670 is
seen shunting
at the east end
of Edinburgh
Waverley in steam
days.

BR 0-6-0 diesel
No. D3728 is seen
shunting at the east
end of Edinburgh
Waverley.

The royal train hauled by A4 4-6-2 Pacific No. 60009 *Union of South Africa* waits to depart Edinburgh's Waverley station on the opening of the Borders Railway on 9 September 2015.

Ex-LMS Stanier Black Five 4-6-0 locomotive No. 45157 *The Glasgow Highlander* departs Edinburgh Waverley for Tweedbank on a SRPS Fife Coast–Scottish Border Tour on 26 August 2018.

Flying Scotsman is seen at the head of the 13.36 *The Cathedral Express* Fife Circular Tour. The train has just arrived back at Edinburgh Waverley from Tweedbank on 20 May 2018.

Ex-LMS 4-6-0 loco No. 46100 *Royal Scot* is seen departing Edinburgh Waverley on the 09.54 train to Tweedbank on Sunday 18 September 2016.

The site of the entrance to Scotland Street tunnel, which can be seen in Edinburgh Waverley.

Bonnington Junction – North Leith (North British Railway)

Above: BR 0-4-0 diesel No. D2720 is seen at Bonnington Square Crossing on 4 March 1959.

Right: Bonnington South signal box seen on 21 July 1968.

Left: BR 0-6-0 Class 08 diesel No. D3878 is seen passing Bonnington South Junction on 20 August 1961. Chancelot Flour Mill can be seen in the background.

Below: Bonnington station, Newhaven Road, looking west. This station still exists and can be seen on the cycle path/walkway to Leith.

Bonnington station in Newhaven Road seen in 2017.

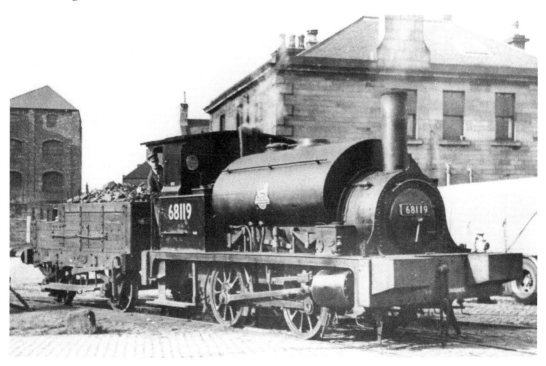

BR 0-4-0ST Class Y9 (ex-NBR) No. 68119 is seen shunting in Bonnington goods yard.

BR 0-4-0ST
Class Y9
(ex-NBR)
No. 68119
is seen in
Bonnington
goods yard.
Bowling Green
Street signal box
can be seen in
the background.

Bowling Green
Street signal box
with Tay Works
with reduced
chimney in
background.

A view of
Junction Bridge
station looking
west.

JUNCTION BRIDGE WIDENING 1909.

Above: In 1909 the bridge at Junction Bridge was widened. The tunnel in the background led to North Leith station (Leith Citadel).

Right: Junction Bridge signal box (LNER) showing air-raid damage sustained on 7 April 1941.

A view of the damage at Junction Bridge station (LNER) caused by German bombs on 7 April 1941.

Another view of the damage sustained at Junction Bridge station (LNER) on 7 April 1941.

Damage sustained to the tenements at Largo Place above Junction Bridge station (LNER) on 7 April 1941.

Junction Bridge station around 1952. The State cinema can be seen in the background. Although this has since been demolished to make way for flats, the front of the cinema has been retained.

Tunnel under Coburg Street with the line to North Leith station (Leith Citadel).

NBR locomotive No. 297 with a train for Edinburgh is seen at North Leith with driver G. W. Kay and fireman L. Gibb.

NBR 4-4-0T loco
No. 273 is seen
at North Leith
station with driver
J. Kay and fireman
Jock McIntosh,
1904.

Ex-NBR now
LNER 4-4-0T loco
No. 10467 is seen
at North Leith
with a train to
Edinburgh on 19
March 1927.

A general view
of North Leith
station pre-1948.
This area is now
occupied by
houses.

BR Class C16 4-4-2T (ex-NBR) No. 67492 is seen on a railtour at North Leith on 6 September 1956.

The outside of North Leith station seen in LNER days.

Railway Society of Scotland railtour is seen at what was left of North Leith (Leith Citadel) station on 7 October 1967.

BR 0-6-0 J37 (ex-NBR) No. 64577 is seen rejoining the main line at Bonnington South Junction.

BR 0-4-0 diesel No. D2721 (NBL) is seen leaving the ex-NBR North Leith branch on 27 March 1967 at Bonnington South Junction.

Princes Street – Davidson's Mains – Barnton – Crew Junction – Granton Gas Works – Granton – Leith North (Caledonian Railway)

A rare picture of a deserted Princes Street station known locally as 'the Caley'. The figure in the picture is Robert Currer, who formally retired as Traffic Superintendent of the CR's Western District on 10 January 1901.

Ex-Caledonian Railway's loco No. 123 on a Special SLS-BLS railtour is seen at Princes Street station on 19 April 1965.

The vehicular entrance to the former CR's Edinburgh Princes Street station, which can still be seen in Rutland Street.

Dalry Road station in the 1950s.

Dalry Middle Junction, 29 February 1964. The Granton & Leith branch line is off to the right while the Dalry Western branch is off to the left.

Edinburgh Tram No. 38 bound for Edinburgh Zoo is seen passing under the former CR bridge at Roseburn carrying the lines to Granton and Leith.

BR 3F 0-6-0 (ex-CR Class 812) No. 57559 is seen at Murrayfield station with a train for Leith North. Remnants of the old station platforms can still be seen.

Another view of Murrayfield station, 1960.

Two BR locos Nos 73062 and 73063 are seen heading a Glasgow–Murrayfield 'Rugby Special' through Craigleith station on 19 March 1960. Having deposited the fans at Murrayfield station, the train is proceeding Empty Coaching Stock (ECS) to Leith North.

BR 2P 0-4-4T (ex-CR Class 439) No. 55202 at Craigleith station on a train for Princes Street station.

Craigleith station looking north on 11 January 1958.

Above: Craigleith Junction, 1958. The line to the left is the Barnton branch.

Right: Davidson's Mains Goods Yard. This site is now a supermarket car park.

A murky view of Davidson's Mains station looking towards Barnton.

Davidson's Mains Railway station (Barnton Gate) with a train for Barnton seen in CR days.

The official opening of the Caledonian Railway's Barnton (Cramond Brig) station on 1 March 1894. It was opened by Sir James Maitland.

A view of Barnton station on 2 October 1946.

The last train from
Barnton station,
7 May 1951.

The outside of
Barnton station, 1950.

A general view of
Crew Junction.

Crew Junction looking north. The Granton branch is seen going off to the left, while the Leith branch is off to the right.

An aerial view of Crew Junction and surrounding area.

The opening of Granton Gas Works station, 27 February 1903, with 812 Class CR No. 821.

Granton Gas Works station currently being redeveloped.

The clock on Granton Gas Works station still working today.

Edinburgh Corporation Gas Department 0-4-0 locomotive No. 6 is seen at Granton Gas Works. New to the Gas Works, the loco was scrapped from there in 1965.

Ex-Scottish Gas Works, Granton Works, 0-4-0 loco No. 10 is seen at Boat of Garten on the Strathspey Railway, 1974.

Scottish Gas Works, Granton Works, 2-foot 0-4-0 locomotive No. 5 seen inside the Gas Works.

Ex-CR Granton High Goods station seen in BR days.

The former CR Granton High Goods station, which is today used by William Waugh, scrap merchant.

BR 3F 0-6-0 (ex-CR No. 298 Class 300) loco No. 57654 has just left Granton and is seen heading west on 12 March 1955.

BR 0-6-0 Class J35 (ex-NBR) No. 64495 on a freight train passing Breakwater Junction signal box on its way from Granton lower yard to Crew Junction. Texaco Oil Terminal is to the left.

A BR oil train leaving Granton Square heading up to Texaco Oil Terminal beside Granton Gas Works on the remains of the former CR line.

The Texaco Oil Terminal sidings beside the former CR line, with a train picking up a load of aviation fuel.

BR 0-6-0 J37 (ex-NBR) loco No. 64624 is seen leaving Granton Square on the former CR Granton branch with a railtour on 31 August 1963.

A Leith-bound DMU pauses at East Pilton Halt, which opened on 1 December 1934 to serve the expanding housing development at East Pilton. Bruce Peebles factory can be seen in the background.

A snowy Granton Road station is seen on 26 February 1955.

Edinburgh trams Nos 158 and 312 on services 27 to Firrhill and 14 to Church Hill are seen outside the former CR Granton Road station on 3 August 1953.

The station was the terminus for the service 27 to Firrhill as well as the service 23, which went to the former NBR Morningside Road station.

Newhaven Junction, the Leith New Lines, can be seen branching off to the left. The freight-only lines can be seen to the right in the picture.

The signal box at Newhaven Junction.

A general view of Newhaven station. The freight lines can be seen in the background.

Track workers at
Newhaven station.

BR 0-6-0 J38 (ex-NBR)
with a train for Leith
North waits to depart
Newhaven station.

The former CR yard at
Lindsay Road (Leith
North), 22 June 1934.

Leith North signal box.

BR 0-4-4T (ex-CR) No. 55165 with a train for Edinburgh Princes Street station, July 1954.

Former CR, now British Railways, Leith North Passenger station, possibly early 1960s as old tramlines can still be seen in the foreground. This area is now called Ocean Terminal, where the royal yacht *Britannia* is permanently berthed and open to the public.

Left: The last train from Leith North station on 28 April 1962.

Below: Road bridge at North Fort Street, Leith, over the entrance to the former CR goods yard at Lindsay Road and Leith North station, 26 December 2017.

Leith Central Station
(North British Railway)

A general view of Lochend Junction with railway lines going to Abbeyhill, Edinburgh Waverley, Granton and Leith Central. The Murray Park Maltings sidings can be seen in the left of the picture.

The signal box at Lochend Junction on 21 July 1968.

Piershill station, July 1967.

Piershill Junction signal box, 21 April 1956.

Above: Manchester, Sheffield & Lincolnshire Railway wooden-bodied carriage No. 946 is seen on display in Leith on 10 November 2018 to commemorate the end of the First World War. This was the type of carriage that was used to carry the troops involved in the Gretna rail disaster in 1915.

Right: Gretna Railway Disaster Memorial, Rosebank Cemetery, not long after it was erected.

James (Jimmy) Gordon, station foreman, Leith Central.

YOUR REF.		BRITISH TRANSPORT COMMISSION	OUR REF.	A.3274.	B.R. 3/2
DATED		BRITISH RAILWAYS	DATE	28.6.55.	
		Scottish. REGION			

TO **District** Station Foreman, J. Gordon, Leith Central.

(Centre No.)

FROM

Station Master, Abbeyhill.

Extn............

(Centre No.)

Leith Central : Engine No. 61402 Derailed : 22.6.55.

I have to inform you that you were at fault in waving the Driver of the engine forward, while the signal was in the "On" position, and I have to warn you that you will require to exercise greater discretion in future when dealing with shunting movements where signals are concerned, while no further action is being taken I would remind you that very serious notice will be taken should there be a repitition.

Telegram sent to James Gordon from the stationmaster at Abbeyhill.

PERSONAL

MR J. GORDON

STATION FOREMAN

LEITH CENTRAL STATION.

Envelope addressed to James Gordon, station foreman, Leith Central station.

South Leith station, Constitution Street, Leith, formerly Edinburgh & Dalkeith Railway station, closed in 1903 following the opening of Leith Central. This was the residence of the late James Gordon, station foreman, Leith Central.

A view of South Leith station, Constitution Street, Leith, looking east.

NBR bell from the
ex-Edinburgh &
Dalkeith South Leith
station.

Leith Central station, opened 1 July 1903. Driver H. Ramage, Fireman W. Paxton.

Left: NBR 4-4-0T No. 33 is seen at Leith Central with driver Jimmy Kay and fireman Jock McIntosh.

Below: A view looking north from Hawkhill Avenue along the Leith Central branch. The bridge carrying the former CR Leith New Lines can be seen in the foreground.

The train entrance to Leith Central station seen on 2 January 1970.

Inside a rather derelict-looking Leith Central station, 1955.

The interior of Leith Central station showing the vastness of the station, 1960.

The outside of Leith Central station seen on 27 November 2016.

On the Leith Central branch there was a halt for football specials calling at Easter Road, the home of Hibernian Football Club. Return trains left from Abbeyhill station.

Another view of Easter Road Park Halt (Hibernian Football Stadium) with James Dunbar Aerated Lemonade factory in the background.

Newhaven Junction – Leith Walk – Easter Road – South Leith Goods (Caledonian Railway – Leith New Lines)

Leaving Newhaven Junction, the CR's Leith New Lines ran south through Victoria Park, Newhaven, before heading south-east to Leith. Trinity Academy can be seen off to the right.

The cutting today. All that remains of the old line is the bridge in Newhaven Road.

Edinburgh tram on service 14 to Church Hill passing the site of Ferry Road station, which was previously occupied by Pratt Brothers, an electrical company. The site is now a block of flats.

A view looking south of the platforms at Ferry Road station, 22 June 1934, which never opened to passenger traffic.

Another view looking north of Ferry Road station.

Bowstring Girder Bridge carrying the Leith New Lines across Bonnington Haughs.

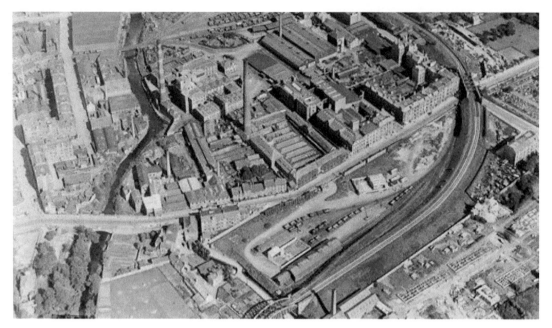

An aerial view showing the Leith New Lines at Bonnington Toll. The goods yard at Rosebank is also visible.

The first of three girder bridges carrying the line over Bonnington Toll. Various types of bridges, as well as viaducts, were constructed to carry the CR elevated line through Leith.

The second of three bridges constructed to carry the line through Leith. The bridge is seen carrying the line over Leith Walk in August 1968.

A view from the top of the bridge over Leith Walk looking west, April 1968.

BR 0-6-0 Class J37 (ex-NBR) No. 64624 is seen at the head of a railtour at Leith Walk station on 31 August 1963. This station was never completed and like Ferry Road never saw regular passenger service. Parts of the original station still exist.

A general view of Leith Walk station looking west, 31 August 1963.

A view looking east from the top of the former Leith Walk station today.

A view of the remains of the ex-CR bridge and station in Leith Walk on 27 November 2016.

Part of the viaduct that once carried the Leith New Lines to Seafield seen in Manderston Street on 16 November 2019.

The third and last of the big girder bridges crossing Easter Road, August 1968. Note the bridge in the background leading to Leith Central station (ex-NBR).

Part of the former trackbed and road bridge over the Leith New Lines at Lochend.

Part of the former trackbed and road bridge over the Leith New Lines at Restalrig, where there was a goods yard.

Builder's plate on the bridge at Restalrig.

Bridge carrying the Leith New Lines across Seafield Road at the entrance to Seafield Crematorium and Cemetery.

Edinburgh trams on a special excursion passing below the bridge carrying the Leith New Lines over Seafield Place, Leith. Bernard's Maltings can be seen in the background.

BR 0-6-0 Class J37 (ex-NBR) No. 64624 is seen at Leith East goods yard on 31 August 1963 having arrived with a railtour.

BR 0-6-0 Class J37 (ex-NBR) No. 64624 ready to depart Leith East goods yard.

BR 4MT 2-6- 0 No. 76106 is seen shunting at Leith East goods yard.

A colour view of Leith East, November 1973.

A goods train headed by BR 0-6-0 loco No. 57654 (ex-CR) from Leith East is seen coming off the former CR's Leith New Lines at Newhaven Junction, heading west.

South Leith Yard
(North British Railway)

Leith South Junction signal box seen on 20 April 1967. The guard's van in the background appears to be in a bit of trouble.

The entrance to the Freight Depot, Leith South.

Seafield yard where an engine shed can be seen in the background. This facility was built by the Caledonian Railway but because the expected dock traffic never materialised the yard proved surplus to requirements. The yard and engine shed were leased to the NBR, who never used it. The yard and engine shed were brought into use in 1945 by the LNER for storing locomotives as there was no spare capacity at St Margaret's Shed at Meadowbank.

BR 0-4-0ST Class Y9 (ex-NBR) No. 68095 is seen at Seafield, August 1955.

South Leith yard, with Seafield Road to the left and ex-CR line to Leith East on the far left.

BR 0-6-2T Class N15 (ex-NBR) Nos 69173 and 69141 are seen departing South Leith with a coal train on 26 May 1956.

BR 0-6-0T Class N15 (ex-NBR) No. 69186 is seen at Seafield Road.

BR 0-6-0T Class N15 (ex-NBR) No. 69149 passing Meadows signal box.

Kings Road Junction signal box.

Leith Docks

The crew of BR 0-4-0ST Class Y9 (ex-NBR) No. 68092 rest between shunting duties at Leith Docks.

EWS Class 66242 is seen pushing an empty coal train into Leith Docks to pick up imported Polish coal for the now closed Cockenzie Power Station on 18 February 2007.

Miscellaneous

BRITISH RAILWAYS

DIESEL
TRAIN SERVICE
AND
CHEAP TRAVEL FACILITIES

CRAIGLEITH   GRANTON ROAD
DALRY ROAD   LEITH (NORTH)
EAST PILTON   MURRAYFIELD
and NEWHAVEN

WITH

EDINBURGH (Princes Street)
12th September 1960 to 10th June 1961
(or until further notice)

Commercial Representatives
are available to assist and advise you with your arrangements, or further information can be supplied on application to stations, accredited Rail Ticket Agencies, or J. Y. Comrie, District Commercial Manager, 23 Waterloo Place, Edinburgh. Tel. No. WAVerley 2477.

TRAVEL BY TRAIN

Notice as to Conditions:— Tickets are issued subject to the British Transport Commission's published Regulations and Conditions applicable to British Railways, exhibited at their Stations or obtainable free of charge at station ticket offices.

CHEAP SECOND CLASS FARES — BY ANY TRAIN — ANY DAY

From LEITH (North)

To	Single	Return
Craigleith	7d.	1/1
Dalry Road	7d.	1/2
East Pilton	4d.	8d.
Edinburgh (Princes Street)	7d.	1/2
Granton Road	4d.	8d.
Murrayfield	7d.	1/2

From GRANTON ROAD

To	Single	Return
Craigleith	7d.	9d.
Dalry Road	4d.	1/-
Edinburgh (Princes Street)	4d.	1/-
Leith (North)	4d.	8d.
Murrayfield	4d.	1/-

From CRAIGLEITH

To	Single	Return
Dalry Road	4d.	7d.
East Pilton	4d.	8d.
Edinburgh (Princes Street)	4d.	8d.
Granton Road	5d.	7d.
Leith (North)	7d.	1/1
Newhaven	4d.	1/-

From DALRY ROAD

To	Single	Return
Craigleith	4d.	8d.
East Pilton	4d.	8d.
Granton Road	4d.	1/-
Leith (North)	7d.	1/2
Newhaven	7d.	1/2

From EAST PILTON

To	Single	Return
Craigleith	4d.	8d.
Dalry Road	7d.	1/2
Edinburgh (Princes Street)	7d.	8d.
Leith (North)	4d.	8d.
Murrayfield	7d.	1/2
Newhaven	7d.	1/2

From MURRAYFIELD

To	Single	Return
East Pilton	4d.	8d.
Edinburgh (Princes Street)	4d.	8d.
Granton Road	4d.	1/-
Leith (North)	7d.	1/2
Newhaven	7d.	1/2

From EDINBURGH (Princes Street)

To	Single	Return
Craigleith	4d.	8d.
East Pilton	4d.	8d.
Granton Road	7d.	1/-
Leith (North)	4d.	8d.
Murrayfield	7d.	1/2
Newhaven	7d.	1/2

The above fares are liable to alteration without further notice. Passengers may alight at any intermediate station on surrender of tickets.
First Class Return Tickets are issued at approximately 50% over the above fare.

The tickets are valid on the date for which issued.
*—Valid for 3 days.

BR 35031/40 AF Sept. 1960 Stafford, Netherfield.

Edinburgh Princes Street (the Caley) to Leith North Timetable 1960–1961.

Acknowledgements

I would like to thank the following for the use of their photographs featured in this book, as well as anyone else I may have missed.

The late J. L. Stevenson
Hamish Stevenson
Archie Foley
R. W. Lynn
Peter Stubbs
John Dickson
W. S. Sellar
G. N. Turnbull
Graeme Fraser
David Dickson
Brian Dishon
Bill Jamieson

With special thanks to Douglas Yuill for the use of his pictures and assistance.

To see further pictures of the railways in Edinburgh, Granton and Leith please visit my website, trainbuff.net.

Kenneth G. Williamson,
Edinburgh